STREET POEMS

STREET

P
O
E
M
S

by   Robert Froman

The McCall Publishing Company   •   New York

To Wendy Partridge and Ruth Spitzer,
first readers extraordinary

S T R E E T   P O E M S

Copyright © 1971 by Robert Froman
Published simultaneously in Canada by Doubleday Canada Ltd., Toronto.
SBN 8415-2025-9
Library of Congress Catalog Card Number: 79-135441
First Printing
Printed in the United States of America
The McCall Publishing Company
230 Park Avenue
New York, New York 10017

CONTENTS

STREET POEMS

UNDEFEATED

A   little   square   of   earth

The   sidewalk   forgot   to   cover.

Lost.

Alone.

Until |ı| weeds |ı| start ı|ı coming |ı| up.

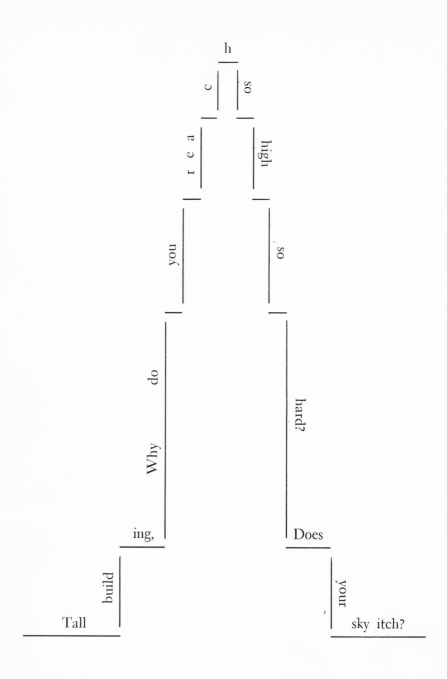

SKYSCRATCHER

PUBLIC LIBRARY

Up three

worn

steps,

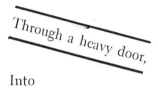

Through a heavy door,

Into

the midst

of books.

From them, anything.

From here, anywhere.

APPETIZER

Corner stand,

Hamburgers frying.

No m a t t e r   h o w   m u c h   o f   i t   I

b   r   e   a   t   h   e,

Istillfeelhungry.

Quiet.

Empty.

Echoes.

D i s m a l ?

P
e
a
c
e
f
u
l
?

NO PRETENDING

DANDELION, NO
BRIGHT DANDELIO

You

are

not

for

any-

thing,

You

just

are.

DANCE

Washing on the line.

Here comes the wind.

FLAP NOW!

FLAP

FLAP

FLAP

FLAP

FLAP

FLAP

FLAP

FL

F

L

EASY DIVER

Pigeon on the roof.

Dives.

Go-

ing

fa-

st.

G

O

I

N

G

T

O

HIT HARD!

Opens wings.

Softly,   gently,

down.

SOLID

Man building a brick wall.

One brick on top of another.

And another. And another.

THE CITY QUESTION

Wino? Junkie?
on sidewalk. Hurt?
face Sick?
on Knife
Man in
pocket?

Danger?

Medicine
in
pocket?
die May
without
it?

Forget
him?

Leave

him

to

the

cops?

Or try to help?

CITY THUNDER

Storm.

Bright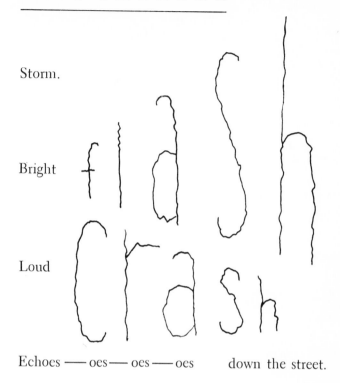

Loud

Echoes —— oes —— oes —— oes   down the street.

Rumblesrumblesrumbles over the roofs.

And slowly grumbles back up into the sky.

NOTHINGEST

Doorway full of d i r t

And t o r n p a p e r.

Window full of

blank.

An empty store.

ORDERS

"DON'T WALK."

"   "

"DON'T WALK."

"   "

"DON'T WALK."

That sign talks too much.

Makes y o u _have_ t o   W   A   L   K.

H O P ^P E R

Sparrow on the walk.

Looking.

^p
Hop ing.

Looking.

Crumbs!

Peck. Peck. Peck. Peck.

OFF AND AWAY

Little piece of paper on the ground.

Going nowhere.

Doing nothing.

Flat.

Little puff of wind.

oop
oo
oo
oo
o
oo
oooo
ooo
o
o
ooooooooooo
oo
oo
oooooo
ooo
o
Sw

FRIENDLY

Beer can in the gutter,

You

at me.

All right.

I'll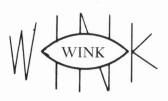

back.

SUPERSTINK

Big bus at the bus stop.

Ready to go again.

Big noise.

Big cloud of

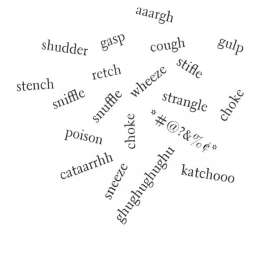

CATCHERS

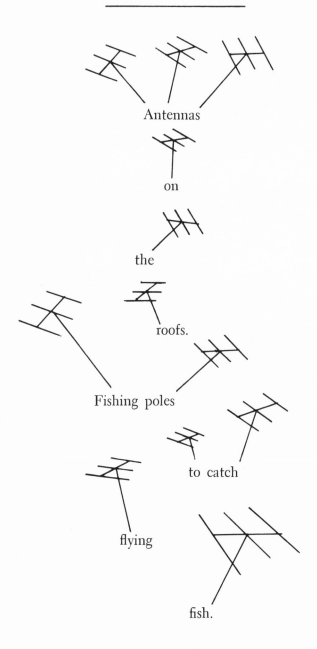

Antennas

on

the

roofs.

Fishing poles

to catch

flying

fish.

COUNTER SERVICE

Stools   straight   in   a   row.

People   straight   on   the   stools.

Faces   straight   on   the   people.

> Carefully,
>
> Fearfully,
>
> Correctly,
>
> Precisely,
>
> Nervously,
>
> Rigidly,
>
> Blankly,
>
> Unhappily,
>
> Prudently,
>
> Guardedly,
>
> Gingerly,
>
> Anxiously,
>
> Straight
>
> Faces.

WINTER WALK

Cold sky, cold air, cold sidewalk, cold street.

Cold.

SHIVERS.

GOOSE pimples.

RuuuBBB HAAANDDDS.

STAMP FEET.

STILL COLD.

GO IN THIS STORE A MINUTE.

AHHHH HHHH!

SURGERY ?

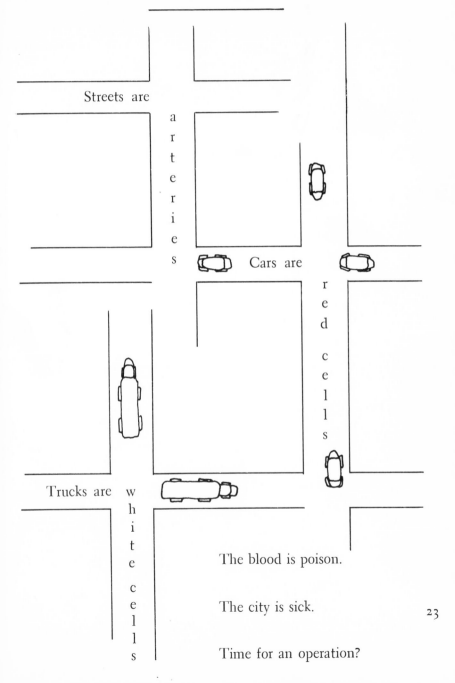

Streets are

arteries

Cars are

red cells

Trucks are white cells

The blood is poison.

The city is sick.

Time for an operation?

23

BLAH-BLAH

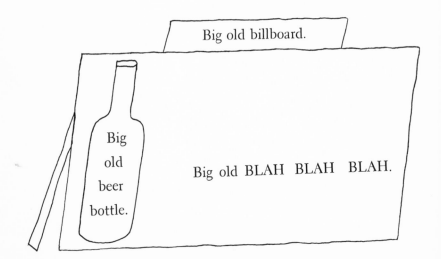

Big old billboard.

Big
old
beer
bottle.

Big old BLAH BLAH BLAH.

AIMLESS

I c i c l e

h a n g i n g

from

the

edge of the roof,

You can't fool me.

You aren't aiming at anyone.

TABLE DEPORTMENT

S t a n d   s t i l l,   t a b l e.

Hold your tablecloth straight.

Keep

your

legs

still.

Once you learn how, table,
This will be easy for you.
It is what you do best.

IGNORED

Down the street a dog barking,

Bragging to a cat in a window.

The cat isn't interested.

MEMORIES

This bro
      ken pla
          te,

What it has held—

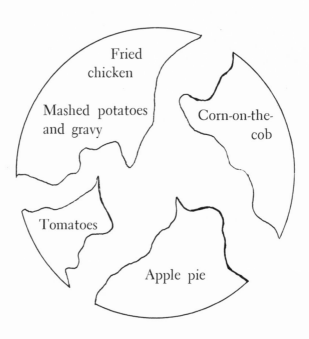

Fried
chicken

Mashed potatoes
and gravy

Corn-on-the-
cob

Tomatoes

Apple pie

Ah.

ON HIS WAY

Butterfly in the gutter.

A crash landing.

A wing broken.

Sad.

No!

There he goes again.

NO SALE

Scccrrrrubbb it, scccrrrrubbb it, scccrrrrubbb it.

Waaasssshhhh it, waaasssshhhh it, waaasssshhhh it.

Cleanit, cleanit, cleanit, cleanit, cleanit, cleanit.

Teevee man wants me to buy his soap.

He wants me to a lot.

My, how he wants me to buy.

But I'm not that dirty.

ROLL, RIVER, ROLL

Keep rolling along,

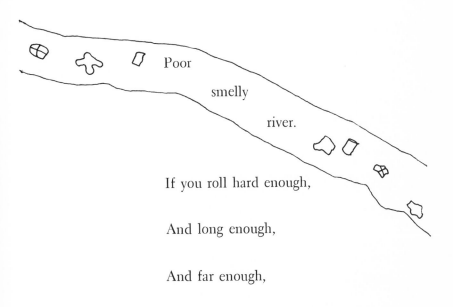

Poor

smelly

river.

If you roll hard enough,

And long enough,

And far enough,

Maybe you can roll yourself clean.

MEANLIGHT

Street lamp,

Stop

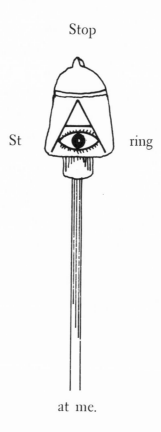

St   ring

at me.

Don't you ever blink?

THE GO-GO GOONS

Cars and trucks at the red light.

Waiting.

Waiting.

Waiting.

Green!

VROOM VROOM V

GREEDY

Big pile

of

orange peels
moldy bread
coffee grounds old shoes tin cans
apple cores meat scrap burned bones
soggy cardboard grease
smashed board toy car broken glass carrot tops
potato peelings banana skins glass jars
envelopes headless doll dead rat

Here comes the garbage truck.

GOBBBBLLLLLE.

L O U D

Tin sign swinging in the wind.

Whack it.

BOINGGGGGGGGGGGGGGGGGGGG

Candy bar—

```
        o l a t e c h o c o l a t e c h o c
      o                                       o
   c        pea-   pea-  pea-   pea-            l
   o    pea- nuts  nuts  nuts   nuts  pea-       a
   h    nuts                          nuts pea-  t
   c        m  a  r  s h m a l l     nuts        e
   c    pea-  m     caramel caramel caramel  w  pea-  e
   h    nuts   m  a                        w  nuts    t
   o    pea-      r  s h m a l l  o  w    pea-  pea-   a
   c    nuts  pea-                        nuts nuts    l
      o      nuts  pea-  pea-  pea-  pea-            c
        l a t e c h o c o l a t e c h o c
```

Too much.

Too much.

But I'll have one more.

SECRETS

lie low, grass blades.

lie still.

whisper to each other.

F A K E

Banners flying.

Lights revolving.

Music playing.

Good time for everyone?

No.

Used car lot.

WAITING

FIREPLUG
YOU LOOK SO
BLANK

SQUATTING

T H E R E

D O I N G

NOTHING

L I K E A

B O M B

WAITING TO

EXPLODE YOUR WATER   39

SUBWAY DEAF

EXPRESS SLAMS PAST THE LOCAL STOP.

MY

   EARS

      SLOWLY

         GET

            READY

to hear again.

HAIL, POLLUTERS

Motor exhaust

    Chimney smoke

       Oil refiners

          Chemical plants

             Burning garbage

               Tobacco fumes—

You give

The air

An edge

That hurts

Whenever

I try

To breathe it.

UPRIGHT

Stand straight, tree.

Don't try to
       touch

          your

             branches

           to

     your

roots.

You'll
    b
      r
        e
   a
    k

something.

ON THE JOB

Tick it,   Tock it,

Tick it,   Tock it,

Tick it,   Tock it,

Tick it,   Tock it,

Keep ticking   And tocking

Clock.   Don't

Lose   Track.

M A D

Tank truck,

Full of oil,

You keep that stuff all for yourself, tank.

Be selfish.

Hold it tight.

Spill just one drop

And we.

SMASH YOU.

In the windy dark

flying

ghosts?

Oh.

No.

Pieces of newspaper.

G L I D E R

Brown leaf

falling

from

a tree,

T
  w
 i
s
t,
  t
   u

  r
   n—

this way,

that

way.

Have a nice glide down.

RESTING IN PEACE

Junked car.

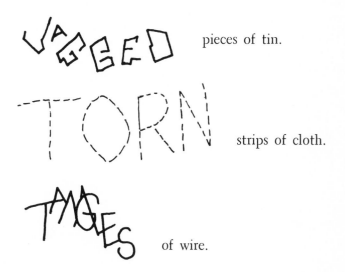

JAGGED   pieces of tin.

TORN   strips of cloth.

TANGLES   of wire.

But you're quiet now, car.

And you don't smell bad.

I like you better dead.

B L O W   U P

higher

and

Wind

around   higher

the

and

corner,

Blow   higher

and

the

high

up

dust

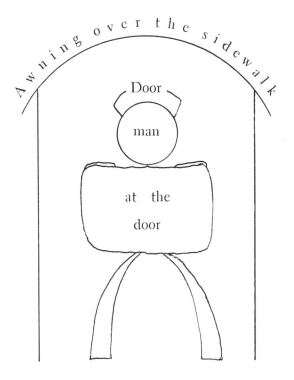

Awning over the sidewalk

Door

man

at the

door

Abandon faith in your fellow man,

Abandon hope for your fellow man,

Abandon charity to your fellow man,

All ye who enter here.

HARDROCK

Big,

High,

Stone

Wall.

Don't try to be soft, wall.

Be hard.

Be cold.

Be heavy.

PUZZLE

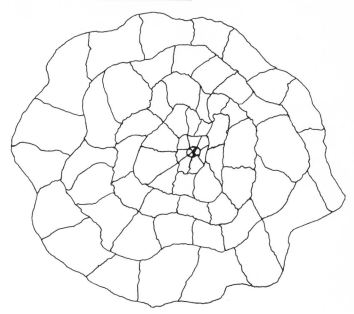

Map of a city with streets meeting at center?

Net to catch people jumping from a burning building?

Spider's web?

Burner on an electric stove?

Fingerprint?

No.

Frozen puddle after a hit by a rock.

COVER UP

The fog.

It hides a lot.

But it doesn't make anything smell better.

S S e r v i c e S S t a t i o n

Stenches of gasoline.

𝐒𝐌𝐄𝐀𝐑𝐒 of grease.

Hissssssss of stale air.

𝐒𝐇𝐑𝐄𝐃𝐒 of tires.

Snarlsssss of don't care.

Lessons in hate-all.

AWAKE AND ASLEEP

Huh?

I'm awake.

Window open.

No light yet.

Everything quiet.

Scary.

Sun up soon.

I'll wait to see it coming up.

Aw.

Daylight.

Missed it again.

H U M B L E W E E D S

Vacant lot full of

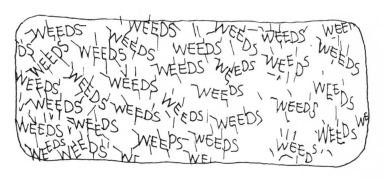

Bow low, weeds.

Cover yourselves with dust.

That way, no one will bother you.

SCARE

Noise in the night—

z
z   z
Click.

z   z   z

Danger?

z   z   z z

Somebody breaking lock?

z z z z z z z z z

Or window?

z z z z z z z z z z

Junkie?

z z z z z z z z z z

Burglar?

z z z z z z z z z z

Hater man?

z z z z z z z z z z z

Ah.

z z z z z z z z z z

Refrigerator.

z z z z z z z z z z

V I E W

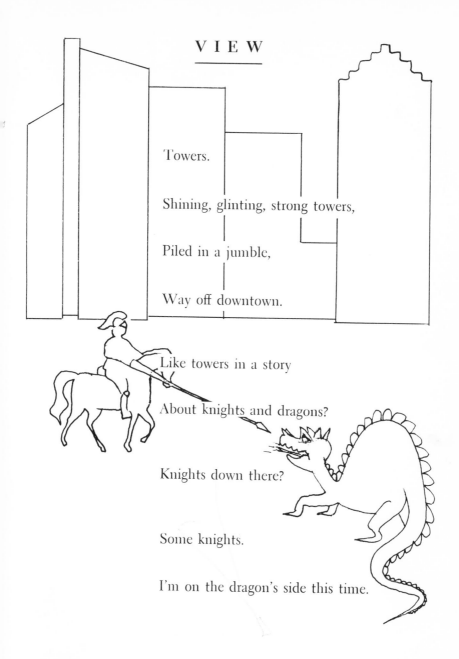

Towers.

Shining, glinting, strong towers,

Piled in a jumble,

Way off downtown.

Like towers in a story

About knights and dragons?

Knights down there?

Some knights.

I'm on the dragon's side this time.

ROOFER

alone on the roof

A P L A N E F L I E S O V E R

makes me lonelier